Fighter!

Luftwaffe Fighter Planes and Pilots by Werner Held
Foreword by Alfred Price

Prentice-Hall, Inc.,
Englewood Cliffs, N.J.

First American edition
published by
Prentice-Hall, Inc, 1979
First German – language
edition: *Die deutsche Tagjagd*,
published 1978
© Motorbuch Verlag,
Postfach 1370,
7000 Stuttgart
© Lionel Leventhal Limited, 1979
ISBN 0–13314–260–4
Library of Congress Catalog Card Number: 79–84835

Printed in Great Britain

Contents

Foreword

There have been several picture books on the Luftwaffe that have drawn on the vast collection of wartime photographs held at the Bundesarchiv in Koblenz. But of these *Fighter!* is certainly one of the best. Here, through the eyes of official photographers, we are treated to an intimate look at the men and machines of the German fighter force from the initial victories at the beginning of the war, until the final crushing defeat in 1945 at the hands of the Allies.

Werner Held has selected his photographs carefully, and captioned them with knowledge and skill.

The latter cannot have been an easy task, as I know from experience: the official captions did not survive with the photographs at the Bundesarchiv, and it often requires considerable detective work and minute examination of other shots in the same series to determine when, where and of whom the photographs were taken. Werner Held has done his work well, and I commend him for it.

Alfred Price

Preface

Since I began working on this book I have often been asked why I was writing a book on the Second World War. Well, a great deal has been written and said on the subject, but not much of it can give the post-war generation a clear idea of what the war was like.

There is a good reason why my first book should be about the Luftwaffe – I was always keen on flying. I obtained my A and B gliding certificates when I was 14, and the C certificate a year later. The end of the war saw to it that I got no further than gliding, so I took up an earthbound trade and became a photographer. It was twenty years before I had anything more to do with aviation. The material for this book was available at my place of work. In the Federal Republic's largest archives, where I had worked as head of the photographic department for ten years, lay what had been saved of the negatives taken by German war correspondents during the Second World War. Writers of many nations come here to seek out photographs, and there are almost two million negatives in the collection.

In starting work on this project, my most important tool was a good magnifying glass. I looked out for rare shots.

As the pictures appeared before me in the darkroom, I tried to imagine what the photographer had experienced at the time. I selected photos that showed people jubilant in victory, crushed and sorrowful in defeat, and pictures that testify to the qualities and power of aircraft, the beauty of landscapes and the cruelty of war.

I have written a short historical introduction to each section. For those who lived through it, these will serve as a bridge into the past; they may help the younger generation to understand the photographs better.

Special thanks are due to the following friends and patrons who have helped me to prepare this illustrated volume: K. Ries of Mainz-Finthen, aircraft specialist; H. Ring of Übersee/Chiemsee, chronicler of fighter aviation; E. Obermaier of Munich, fighter aviation expert; Archivrat Dr. M. Haupt of the Bundesarchiv in Koblenz, who made my researches possible; Oberst Erich Hartmann, retired; Oberstleutnant H. J. Jabs, retired; O. Romm; K. Schnörrer; E. Nickolai; and H. Nauroth.

Werner Held

Luftwaffe Units

During the Second World War, the Luftwaffe's chain of command differed from that of the R.A.F. in that the service was divided into Luftflotten, or Air Fleets, each a self-contained air force. There were five Luftflotten, which were responsible for the specific areas in which they operated; for example, during the Battle of Britain, Luftflotte 2's territory was the Low Countries and Eastern France. The Luftflotten were divided into Luftkorps, or Air Corps, although fighter forces were frequently grouped together under a Jagdführer, or Fighter Leader, who coordinated the activities of all fighter units within his Luftflotte.

The organization of the R.A.F., on the other hand, was divided into functional Commands, i.e., Fighter, Bomber, Coastal, Training and Transport. Each of these was led by its own commander (usually an Air Chief Marshal), and comprised self-contained squadrons which were organized into Wings and Groups on a geographical basis. The advantage of this system over the German Luftflotten was that each Command had leaders who were expert in their own branch of operations; a Luftflotte commander was expected to coordinate the activities of widely differing units.

Within the Luftwaffe, the largest flying unit was the Geschwader, which was designated and numbered according to its function, for example Zerstörergeschwader 26 (operating with Bf 110 'Destroyers') or Jagdgeschwader 51 (operating with single-engined fighters). A Geschwader was divided into three, four, or sometimes five Gruppen, each with a nominal strength of thirty aircraft. The Gruppe was the basic unit, somewhat larger than a British squadron, and its component flights were known as Staffeln. A Staffel had nine aircraft plus that of the Staffelkapitän, who was usually an Oberleutnant or Hauptmann. The three or more Kapitäne of a Gruppe flew together as the unit's Stabskette, or Staff Flight. The Kommandeur of a Gruppe was usually a Hauptmann or a Major, whilst a Geschwader was led by a Major, Oberstleutnant, or Oberst, who was known as the Geschwaderkommodore.

Although a Gruppe would usually occupy one airfield and operate as a complete unit, its component Staffeln were self-contained entities with their own traditions, ground crew, badges and occasionally even colour schemes.

Staffeln and Gruppen were numbered as part of their Geschwader. Staffeln were identified by Arabic numbers and Gruppen by Roman, for example 3./JG 54 was the third Staffel of Jagdgeschwader 54; III./ZG 26 was the third Gruppe of Zerstörergeschwader 26, comprising the Gruppe's 7th, 8th and 9th Staffeln. These designations were altered for the Legion Condor during the Spanish Civil War, when the Gruppen were identified as 1.J/88, 2.J/88 and 3.J/88.

Comparative table of ranks.

Luftwaffe	R.A.F.	U.S.A.A.F.
Generalfeldmarschall	Marshal of the R.A.F.	
Generaloberst		
General der Luftwaffe	Air Chief Marshal	General
Generalleutnant	Air Marshal	Lieutenant-General
Generalmajor	Air Vice-Marshal	Major-General
	Air Commodore	Brigadier General
Oberst	Group Captain	Colonel
Oberstleutnant	Wing Commander	Lieutenant Colonel
Major	Squadron Leader	Major
Hauptmann	Flight Lieutenant	Captain
Oberleutnant	Flying Officer	First Lieutenant
Leutnant	Pilot Officer	Second Lieutenant
Feldwebel (Stabs-Haupt-Ober-)	Warrant Officer	Master Sergeant
Unterfeldwebel	Flight Sergeant	First Sergeant
Unteroffizier	Sergeant	Technical Sergeant
Hauptgefreiter	Corporal	Staff Sergeant
Obergefreiter	Leading Aircraftman	Sergeant
Gefreiter	Aircraftman 1st Class	Corporal
Flieger	Aircraftman 2nd Class	Private 1st Class

Additional ranks mentioned in the text are Fähnrich (Ensign or Officer Cadet), Oberwerkmeister (a Chief Engineering Officer or NCO), and Reichsmarschall, a rank held only by Hermann Göring. As the Luftwaffe's ranks were the same as those of the German Army, in the text they have been translated into their British Army equivalents.

The Reconstruction of the German Fighter Arm after the First World War

Through skilful propaganda, a surprised world was convinced, in the early 1930s, that Hitler had been able to produce something as technically involved as an air force, virtually out of a hat. The 1919 Treaty of Versailles had required the surrender or destruction of all available German aircraft. All flying units, even the Police Staffeln, were to be disbanded. The further production in Germany of aircraft or parts of such, including aircraft engines, was prohibited. This restriction was relaxed in 1922, when the production of aircraft for purely civil use was permitted, under the supervision of the occupying powers.

The Rapallo negotiations led to liaison between the German Army, or Reichswehr (limited to 100,000 men) and the Red Army. This permitted the partial circumvention of the restrictions on Germany's military strength by Russia supplying facilities for the development and testing of weapons prohibited under the terms of the Treaty of Versailles.

Thus was founded, at Lipetsk in Russia, a German military flying school where, in addition to the training of service pilots, new aircraft types could be evaluated. Between 1925 and 1933, some 120 officers returned from Lipetsk as fully qualified fighter pilots, able to fly any modern aircraft type after a short conversion course.

In 1926 further relaxations on aircraft construction were introduced. By 1932 the Ar 64 and He 51 fighters had been tested, selected and prepared for series production with an eye to establishing Army flying units; the He 51 was to form part of the initial equipment of Göring's young fighter arm.

At Hitler's behest the Lipetsk establishment, hitherto kept secret, was abandoned. New blood was henceforth to be trained in the Luftsportverband (Air Sport Association). The first fighter pilot school was established at the Deutsche Verkehrsfliegerschule (German Commercial Pilots' School) at Schleissheim. On 26 February 1935 Hitler announced the official formation of the Luftwaffe and all secrecy was finally abandoned. April 1935 saw the inauguration, under Major Ritter von Greim, of the first German Jagdgeschwader (Fighter Geschwader), which bore the title of Jagdgeschwader Richthofen 2. Pilots from this unit were drafted to form further Geschwader. The first Gruppe, flying Arado Ar 65s, was stationed at Döberitz, and the second Gruppe, equipped with He 51s, at Jüterborg Damm. The Bernburg Gruppe was then formed and soon followed by the Aibling Gruppe.

The German fighter arm made its first public appearance during the occupation of the Rhineland on 7 March 1936. The initial equipment of the units was soon replaced by up-to-date products of the growing German aircraft industry, and the Spanish Civil War provided an opportunity to evaluate the new aircraft in actual combat conditions.

The German Luftwaffe had become an independent service alongside the Reichsheer (Army) and Kriegsmarine (Navy.) By the outbreak of war in 1939, German aircraft were at least equal to those of other nations, and better than most. However, this led to complacency and faulty planning, which was later to rebound with disastrous effect.

Top: Final examination for the class of 1931 at the Deutsche Verkehrsfliegerschule (D.V.S.) at Schleissheim, 1932. The ten best pilots out of thirty will go on to fighter training at Lipetsk in Russia. The aircraft are As 10-engined Arado Ar 66 trainers.
Middle: The pilots in this formation of Arado 64s are, from left to right, Radusch, Bollmann, Trautloft, Lützow and Aschmann. The photograph was taken in 1934, by which time the D.V.S., Schleissheim, had been renamed the Jagd Fliegerschule (Fighter Pilot School).
Left: Examination Committee, spring 1932, D.V.S. Schleissheim: left to right, Hauptmann Vierling, retd., Rittmeister Bolle, retd. (a Pour le Mérite ace), and Fluglehrer (Flying Instructor) von Beaulieu.

Top: The 'Richthofen' Jagdstaffel at Döberitz, 3 August 1935. The He 51 was the standard aircraft for the German fighter units during the reconstruction period of the Luftwaffe.
Middle: Arado Ar 68F fighters of 4th Staffel, JG 134 'Horst Wessel' at Jever beim Schiessen in 1936.
Bottom: Swearing-in of recruits at the base for JG 132 'Richthofen' (later renumbered Jg 2).

The occupation of the Rhineland: He 51As of III./Jg 134 over Cologne, 7 March 1936.

Top: The replacement for the He 51 was the Messerschmitt Bf 109B–1.
Middle: A Gruppe takes off from Rechlin. In 1938 the Bf 109D still bore its swastika on a white disc.
Bottom: High jinks! The aircraft is a Bf 109C–2.

Above: Autumn manoeuvres, 1938. Messerschmitt Bf 110
Zerstörer (Destroyer) of ZG 76 in the Mark of Brandenburg.
Below: Bf 109E–2 of I./JG 76 (later II./JG 54)

Above: A tripod-mounted machine gun protects a Bf 109E–1 of 4./JG 132.
Below: Bf 109Ds of the Bernburg Fighter Gruppe. From 1 May 1939, this unit was known as I./ZG 2.

The Legion Condor

The murder of a politician was the spark that ignited the powder keg of Spain in the summer of 1936. A bloody civil war began between Republicans and Nationalists. The Nationalist General Francisco Franco, whose Moro battalions were then stationed in Spanish Morocco, asked the German government for Junkers transports. Hitler supplied not only material help, but also reinforcements; the Hisma transport company was formed and Ju 52s, crewed by Germans, flew the Moros from North Africa to the Iberian Peninsula. This was the first large-scale airlift in history.

In August 1936 the first volunteers of the Legion Condor arrived in Spain. The force comprised a bomber and fighter Gruppe, an enlarged reconnaissance Staffel, three Flak regiments, three air signals units, and a marine Gruppe. The Legion Condor was first led by General Hugo Sperrle, then from November 1937 by Generalmajor Volkmann, and finally from November 1938 by Generalmajor Wolfram von Richthofen, a cousin of the First World War air ace. Three fighter squadrons, equipped with the He 51, became operational in November 1936. 1.J/88, the 'Marabu' Staffel, was led by Oberleutnant Günther Lützow, 2.J/88, the 'Top Hat' Staffel by Oberleutnant Joachim Schlichting, and 3.J/88, the 'Micky Mouse' Staffel, by Oberleutnant Adolf Galland (later by Werner Mölders).

Unfortunately, the He 51 proved to be inferior to the fast and manoeuvrable Curtiss Hawks and Ratas of the Republican Air Force, so in March 1938 2.J/88 was re-equipped with the Messerschmitt Bf 109. 1.J/88 converted soon afterwards and 3.J/88 in September 1938. Until that time, the third Staffel had flown their He 51s against ground targets, but then a fourth Staffel was added, exclusively for ground-attack work. With the Bf 109, the German pilots very quickly gained air superiority. This aircraft remained in service as a standard fighter until the end of the Second World War.

The Legion's bomber and fighter squadrons were always sent to the areas of heaviest fighting, and were known as 'Franco's Fire Brigade'. During the Spanish Civil War, German fighter pilots shot down a confirmed total of 340 enemy aircraft.

'We flew across the borders
To bomb the enemy
High over Spanish soil
With friends from Italy.'
(Legion Condor song)

Above: He 51s near Salamanca, Spring 1937.

Below: Air superiority was easily gained after conversion to the Bf 109.

Top: The Legion Condor on parade after the conclusion of the Spanish Civil War. To the left of the standard is 'Fürst' (Prince) Wilcke, who later became a successful fighter pilot.

Bottom left: The tail of Werner Mölders' Bf 109.

Bottom right: The Legion Condor's three most successful fighter pilots. Left to right: Mölders (fourteen victories), Schellmann (12 victories), and Harder.

Top: A Bf 109 burns after a landing accident.
Bottom left: These Bf 109s, flying over the Sierra, demonstrate the Luftwaffe's proven 'finger four' fighter formation (Schwarm), which was first tried in Spain.
Bottom right: Briefing for a Bf 109 Staffel.

Top: Returning airmen embark at Vigo.

Bottom left: A convoy of 'Kraft durch Freude' ('Strength through Joy') ships in German waters. German troops were ferried to and from Spain in ships posing as State-sponsored pleasure cruisers. Shown here are the 'Sierra Cordoba', the 'Wilhelm Gustloff', the 'Robert Ley' and 'Der Deutsche'.

Bottom right: Hermann Göring receives the Legion Condor in Berlin. He is accompanied (from left to right of the picture) by von Richthofen, Milch and Sperrle.

The Polish Theatre - September 1939

At first light on the morning of 1 September 1939, German troops crossed the Polish border, precipitating the Second World War. Concentrated attacks by horizontal- and dive-bomber units destroyed airfields and supply lines, but the Polish fighters and bombers had moved to well camouflaged emergency airfields before the outbreak of hostilities. The P.Z.L. 11c fighter was hopelessly inferior to the Bf 109, and achieved few successes. Within a week, the Polish Air Force had ceased to exist and, helped by the bomber and close-support Gruppen, the German Army overcame the Polish defenders in eighteen days.

Eight fighter and five Zerstörer (Bf 110) Gruppen shot down about 120 enemy machines – before the war Poland had possessed 396 aircraft, of which 160 were fighters. The Luftwaffe lost 285 machines, most of which fell to Polish anti-aircraft fire during ground attacks.

Below: Hannes Trautloft and his men of IV./JG 132 before the invasion of Poland, 1939. Bf 109E–1 Nr 4072 carries interesting red and white markings on fuselage and spinner.

Above: Despite the political tension during summer 1939, there was always time for a game of 'skat'.

Above: Hubert Kroeck, the commanding officer of 4./JG 53, briefs his pilots. This is probably a staged shot, as briefings are always more conveniently conducted indoors!

Top: Hauptmann Hannes Trautloft with his 2nd Staffel, IV./JG 132 during the Polish campaign.
Middle: Last-minute instructions by telephone.
Bottom: An improvised airfield on the Polish border.

Left: This Bf 109E–3 of L/JG 76 overturned on landing.
Below left: I./JG 1 (later III./JG 27) operated out of East Prussia. In the background are Henschel Hs 123 dive-bombers.

Left: A quick haircut while on alert.
Below left: At the outbreak of war, Hauptmann Günther Lützow was left to defend Berlin with training Staffeln.

Right: A dogfight with Polish P.Z.L. fighters in September 1939, as visualized by the propaganda artist.
Below: German infantry inspect a 'downed' Polish P.Z.L. 11c fighter. Actually, this is a propaganda photograph, staged with a machine captured on the ground.

The Battle of the German Bight

On 4 and 28 September 1939, British Blenheim and Wellington bombers entered German air space over the German Bight and attempted to attack the German fleet. The attacks were beaten off by Flak, many aircraft being shot down. In air-to-air combat, fighter pilots Unteroffizier Held and Feldwebel Troitsch claimed the first British bombers shot down during the Second World War. Undaunted, the British returned to attack the German fleet on 18 December. Machines of 9 and 149 Squadrons, R.A.F., appeared over the Bight in a clear blue sky and proceeded to fly in a wing-to-wing parade-ground formation over Wilhelmshaven. Heavy anti-aircraft fire forced them to turn north-west, and no bombs were dropped. Suddenly, Bf 109s and 110s of Jagdgeschwader 'Schumacher' (JG 1) fell upon the British and broke up the formation, sending several machines down in flames into the North Sea. Leutnant Helmut Lent, who later became a very successful night-fighter pilot, obtained three victories, while Hauptmann Falck, Unteroffizier Fresia,

Leutnant Graeff, Oberleutnant Gresens, Unteroffizier Heilmayr, Unteroffizier Kelinowski, Oberleutnant Robitsch, Oberstleutnant Schumacher, Oberleutnant Steinhoff and Leutnant Üllenbeck were credited with one each. Oberleutnant Gollob claimed a victory that was not confirmed.

The claims issued by both sides that evening differed considerably. While the British claimed twelve German fighters shot down for the loss of seven bombers, the Germans in fact lost only two aircraft. German claims were for thirty-four British bombers. After the war, British reports mentioned twelve losses and a further three crash-landings. No more reliable figures are available, but the battle of the German Bight has gone down in history as the first major aerial engagement of the Second World War. It showed that bombers without a substantial fighter escort were liable to heavy losses. Britain took note; Germany did not.

Right: A war artist's impression of the Battle of the German Bight.

Above: I./ZG 76 on coastal defence duties at Jever.

Top: Bf 109E–3s of II./JG 77 on the island of Wangerooge.

Middle: A pre-war photograph of Bristol Blenheim bombers. This type of aircraft carried out the first raids on German coastal targets, and suffered heavy casualties.

Bottom: Wellington 1As of 149 Squadron, based at Mildenhall, winter 1939–40. The censor appears to have been at work on some of the crews' equipment (Alfred Price).

Top: 4 September 1939: 'Ten Blenheims heading for Wilhelmshaven.' Bf 109 pilots of II./JG 77 check on the bombers' course.
Middle: Two Bf 109Es returning from combat.
Bottom: A boisterous welcome for Unteroffizier (Sergeant) Alfred Held, the first pilot to shoot down a British bomber in the Second World War. (The name Held, incidentally, means 'Hero'.)

Above: A Bf 110C–2 of ZG 26 over the North Sea.
Below: Leutnant Helmuth Lent's third victory in the Battle of the German Bight.

Top: Bf 110s ready for action.
Middle: Kommodore of JG 1,
Oberstleutnant (Lieutenant-Colonel)
Carl Schumacher in his Bf 109E–3.
Bottom: Successful pilots after the
Battle. Second from the left is Gollob,
fourth is Lent and Sixth is Steinhoff.

The Occupation of Norway and Denmark

Scandinavia was the prize in a race. The British planned to land four divisions at Narvik, Drontheim, Bergen and Stavanger. Operation 'Weserübung' was intended to beat them to it. German troopships, escorted by cruisers and destroyers, steamed northwards at full speed to reach their destinations in Norway on 9 April 1940. The airfields at Aalborg, Oslo-Fornebu and Stavanger were captured at a stroke, as paratroops went into action for the first time in history. Five hundred transport aircraft, mainly Ju 52s, ferried paratroops and Alpine troops into Norway and Denmark. Despite initial difficulties, mainly due to foggy weather, the operation succeeded. The airfield at Oslo-Fornebu was first occupied by a Bf 110 Staffel of 1./ZG 76. Leutnant Lent, later to become one of the most successful night-fighter aces, chalked up his fifth victory. Whereas the airfields were taken by surprise, troops landing in the harbours and fjords suffered heavy losses before the Norwegian coastal batteries could be silenced.

Between 14 and 19 April, the British, reinforced by French Foreign Legionnaires and exiled Polish troops, landed at Narvik, Namsos and Andalsnes, near Drontheim. They encountered stubborn resistance, and after two weeks had to be evacuated under a hail of bombs from the Luftwaffe.

The success of the German operation was due to good cooperation between Luftwaffe and Marine, to the element of surprise, and last but not least, to the exceptionally courageous conduct of the ground troops.

Germany's northern flank would remain safe for the rest of the war, and the continued import of iron ore from Sweden was assured.

Below: 109E–2s in Norway.

Above: A picture to commemorate
the dramatic capture of Oslo from
the air. The third pilot from the left is
Helmut Lent.

Above: I./ZG 76 distinguished itself
in the capture of Oslo-Fornebu
airfield. Oberleutnant (First
Lieutenant) Lent, second from the
left, went on to become a famous
night-fighter pilot. The aircraft are Bf
110Cs.

Above: Bf 109Es of JG 77 on a Norwegian airfield.
Left: Servicing a Bf 109E of JG 77.

Top: Norwegian carpenters lay wooden paving on an airfield. The aircraft are Bf 109E–1s.

Middle: Hauptmann Falck talks to General Milch at Aalborg.

Bottom: Bf 109E–3s in a deceptively idyllic setting on the Western Front.

The Western Campaign

After the conquest of Poland, the Western Front settled into the so-called Sitzkrieg, or Phoney War. Germans and Frenchmen watched each other with guns at their feet, while German fighters patrolled the frontier, shooting down the occasional French reconnaissance aircraft. In this way, by May 1940, Haupmann Werner Mölders, the top-scorer in the Spanish War, had added nine victories to his tally.

After several postponements, German troops crossed the borders on 10 May 1940. Airborne assault troops and Fallschirmjäger (paratroops) arrived in gliders behind the Belgian lines and captured the huge fortress of Eben Emael and the Maas and Scheldt bridges. The Dutch, with only a small air force, capitulated on 14 May. The Belgian fighters, despite the courage of their pilots, were no match for the superior Bf 109, and on 18 May the Belgian Army surrendered. Following the style of the Polish campaign, German tanks drove a wedge deep into the French flank. On 14 May hundreds of German and Allied aircraft met near Sedan, the Allies losing over ninety machines. On 3 June French airfields and aircraft factories were destroyed in waves of bombing raids, and on the following day Dunkirk fell, but not before the British had succeeded in evacuating 338,226 men from the beaches.

The French Army was now on its own. The German advance continued and on 14 June Paris was occupied without resistance. Maréchal Pétain, the new head of government, requested an armistice on the 16th. On the 22nd, forty-three days after the invasion started, General Huntziger signed the armistice treaty for France in the forest of Compiègne. A demarcation line separated occupied from unoccupied France. Along the shores of the English Channel fighters, Stukas and bombers moved into new airfields.

The Battle of Britain was about to begin.

A Schwarm of Bf 109Es on border patrol.

Right: Ground crew and Bf 109E–3 of 4./JG 53 in autumn 1939, during the period known as 'The Phoney War'.
Below: A Bf 109C–2 of 2./JG 71 being tanked-up. This unit (on frontier defence duties in 1939) had, for its badge, a rather unkind caricature of the British Prime Minister, Neville Chamberlain.

Right: A belly-landed Bf 109D
near Freiburg, winter 1939–40.
Bottom: Rejoicing over a
victory – still a noteworthy
event in 1939.

Left: Armourers loading the synchronized MG 17s of a Bf 109E.

Right: Hauptmann Werner Mölders wears 'The spanish look', Western Front, September 1939.

Left: A shark-mouthed Bf 109C–2 of I./JG 71 (later II./JG 51).
Below: Quite a hornet's nest of Bf 110C–2s on an airfield in the west, May 1940. The unit is the sole Gruppe of ZG 52, which was absorbed into ZG 2 in July 1940.

Top: Luftwaffe officers
examine a Hurricane
abandoned at Beauvais.
(Alfred Price)
Middle: Foot-sloggers
examine a French Dewoitine
D.520 shot down near Sedan
in May 1940.
Bottom: A Fairey Battle of 150
Squadron which has
crash-landed.

Top: An artist's impression of a Bf 109 in combat with a French Morane-Saulnier M.S. 406.
Above: Fairey Battles await scrapping. The nearest aircraft was from 88 Squadron and the next from 98 Squadron.

Top: French LéO 45 bombers destroyed on the ground.
Middle: Captured French aircraft. From left, M.S. 406, Curtiss 75 Hawk, Bloch 155.
Bottom: A new airfield on the Channel.

The Battle of Britain

The great air battle that went down in history as the Battle of Britain was intended as a preliminary to Unternehmen Seelöwe (Operation 'Sealion'). Before Hitler could attack the Soviet Union, he had to eliminate his last enemy in the west, Great Britain, either by political settlement or by invasion. Three phases were planned before the invasion could take place:

1. The blockade of the British Isles by attacks on shipping and ports, and the mining of harbour entrances and approaches.
2. The attainment of absolute air superiority by eliminating the British fighter arm.
3. The preparation for invasion by means of concentrated large-scale bomber attacks.

At the beginning of the battle, 832 British fighters faced some 700 German single-seater and 200 two-seater fighters. The first phase had already begun during the Battle of France, with the bombing of British supply ships and the mining of harbours. However, further progress was impossible until after the fall of France. Although Stuka units attacked the convoys and were soon able to make the Channel impassable, the Stuka's well-known vulnerability led to ever-increasing losses of the aircraft, which could not even be prevented by increased fighter protection.

The second phase of the battle, the attempt to gain absolute air superiority, petered out in a war of attrition, with heavy losses on both sides. The British Hurricane and Spitfire pilots, however, had several advantages. The German fighters had a limited range, which gave them only twenty minutes of combat time, whereas the British fighters were operating close to their bases and could always retreat out of the range of the Bf 109. British pilots who baled out, or force-landed, were soon back with new machines, whereas German pilots in a similar situation became prisoners. German fighter units flew as many as three cross-Channel sorties daily, but despite the efforts of pilots and ground crew working at full stretch, Germany could not achieve air superiority.

For the third phase, the strategic bombing of targets in London and southern England, the German fighters were required to fly as close escort for the much slower bombers, a task for which their limited endurance made them most unsuitable. Losses amongst both bombers and fighters were high, while the twin-engined Bf 110 heavy fighters proved to be too slow and unwieldy, requiring an escort of their own. Some Gruppen were virtually wiped out, and the third phase was broken off on 7 September 1940.

A further phase was then introduced, and at first some success was achieved by concentrated night-bombing attacks on British armament manufacturing centres. However, losses again began to mount, and the Luftschlacht um England ended on the night of 10/11 May 1941, with a last heavy raid on London. The stated intentions of the campaign had not been achieved, and Operation 'Sealion' did not materialize.

Next stop the British Isles: the British Expeditionary Force monument and Freya radar at Cap Gris Nez.

Left: Hauptmann Günther von Maltzahn, commanding officer of II./JG 53, supervises the painting of the Geschwader's Pik As (Ace of Spades) emblem on a new Bf 109E–4.

Below: Bf 109E–4s take off for a raid on England. These machines have the armoured cockpit canopy introduced in mid-summer 1940.

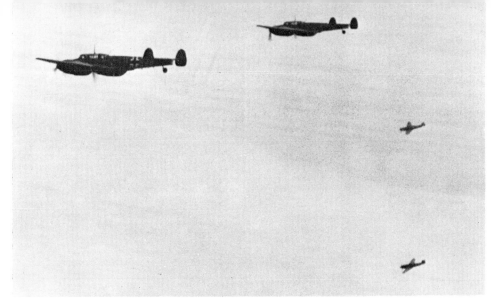

Top: The Bf 110 proved wanting in its intended heavy fighter role, and itself needed a fighter escort.
Middle and bottom: Reichsmarschall Göring visits Cap Gris Nez and looks across the Channel towards Britain.

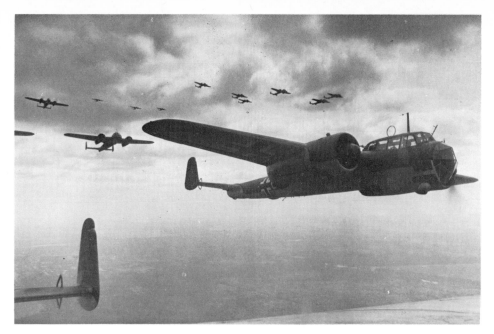

Above: Do 17Z–1 bombers head for England. Göring blames rising losses on the fighter escorts.

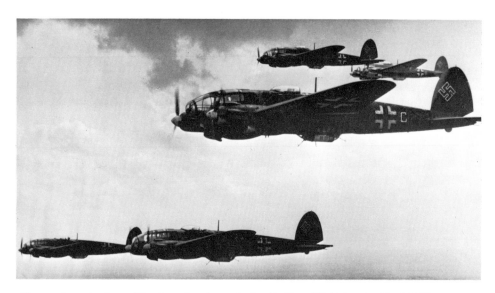

Above: A mainstay of the bomber force in the Battle of Britain, the He 111 (P version shown here) was no more than a medium bomber. The Luftwaffe abandoned the heavy bomber concept in the mid-1930s.

Above: Majors Galland and Mölders with the Reichsmarschall. Göring's private train is parked in the background.

Below: Major Mölders and Hauptmann Wiggers of I./JG 51.

Top: Major Mölders returns from a sortie.
Left: 'There he was, right in front of me . . .'
Adolf Galland describes his latest 'scrap'
to Hauptmann Pingel of I./JG 26. Pingel
force-landed near Dover on 10 July 1941,
and was captured with a total of
twenty-six victories.

Above: The mount of Oberleutnant Heinz Ebeling, Staffelkapitän of 9./JG 26. This pilot amassed eighteen victories before he was forced to bale out over London on 5 November 1940.

Above: Major Galland plans his next bomber escort sortie. JG 26 will lead the formation.

Right: Major Adolf Galland, the commanding officer of II./JG 26, with his crew chief Unteroffizier Meyer, who serviced Galland's aircraft throughout the war. Note the unusual telescopic sight fitted to this machine.

Below: Bf 109E–4s of I./JG 3 are checked-out for an escort sortie, late summer 1940. The aircraft have yellow distempered cowlings and rudders, and armoured canopies.

Top left: Hauptmann Günther Lützow arrives back at Wièvre au Bois, 9 September 1940. His rudder shows thirteen victories.
Top right: In 1940, Leutnant Franz von Werra was Adjutant of II./JG 3. He was later captured by the British and became famous as the only German airman to make a 'home run'. The epic story of his escape across Canada and the U.S.A. was the subject of a film starring Hardy Krüger. He is shown here with Simba, the Gruppe's mascot.
Below: Hauptmann Reinecke of Stab I./ZG 76, about to start up his Bf 110.

Right: The 'ringelpitz' emblem of I./ZG 26 on a Bf 110C. Later in the war, the prey bore both British and Soviet markings.

Below left: Hauptmann Horst Tietzen, Staffelkapitän of 5./JG 51, was shot down after twenty victories on 18 August 1940, and his body was washed ashore near Calais. Note the grave of an unidentified Blenheim crewman in the background.

Below right: Hauptmann Joppien (I./JG 51) received the Ritterkreuz (Knight's cross) on 16 September 1940, after his twenty-first victory.

Top left: JG 26's first Ritterkreuz holders, September 1940. Left to right: Gerhard Schöpfel, Adolf Galland and Joachim Müncheberg.
Top right: 'Uncle Theo' Osterkamp as Jagdführer 1 (Fighter Commander 1) on the Channel coast.
Left: Johann Schalk, Gruppenkommandeur of III./ZG 26, talks tactics in September 1940.

Above: Major Galland and his Bf 109E–4 at Wissant.
Below: 'Hoch soll er leben . . .' ('For he's a jolly good fellow'), celebrating Galland's fortieth victory, 25 September 1940.

Top: This Bf 109E–4 just reached the French coast on its last drop of fuel.

Middle: Others, less lucky, took an unwelcome dip in the Channel. A seaplane crew check a pilot's reported position.

Bottom: Every second counts! The rescuers run to their He 59 B–2. Note the different styles of lifejacket.

Top: The Reichsmarschall visits the fighter units in France. Left to right: Major Galland, General Loerzer, Göring and Major Mölders.

Middle: Göring with an unknown officer, Loerzer and Mölders.

Bottom: Two views of Bf 110C–2s of l./ZG 52 taxiing out. This unit suffered heavy casualties in the latter stages of the Battle of France and the bombing of Channel convoys. By the end of July its survivors had been absorbed into ZG 2, as that Geschwader's Second Gruppe.

Left: Bf 110Cs of ZG 26 en route for England.
Bottom left: Bf 110s peel-off for an attack on a British airfield.
Bottom right: A Bf 110 rear gunner's view of a burning Hurricane. This is probably either a staged or faked propaganda photograph.

Top: Kenley, 18 August, 1940. A Spitfire of 64 Squadron in its blast pen, photographed from a Dornier Do 17 of KG 76.
Middle: Armourers adjust the synchronizing gear of a Bf 109E–4 of 5./JG 54.
Bottom: The Reichsmarschall visits JG 2 'Richthofen' in October 1940. Identified pilots, both with Ritterkreuz, are (left) Assi Hahn and (right) Werner Machold, who was captured in Southern England on 6 June 1941.

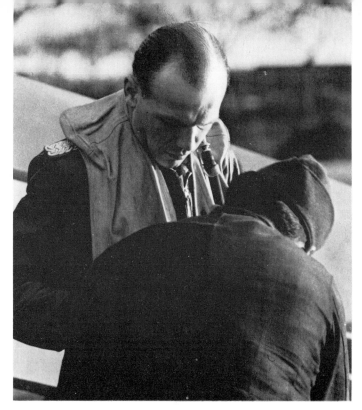

Three photographs of Major Helmut Wick, commanding officer of JG 2, who was one of the Battle of Britain's most successful pilots. He baled out south of the Isle of Wight on 28 November 1940, and was not seen again. The picture at top right was the last ever taken of him. Wick received the Oak Leaves on 10 June 1940 after forty-two victories, and was, with Mölders and Galland one of the three top scorers of the Battle.

Top: Hauptmann Heinz Bretnütz, Kommandeur of II./JG 53, won the Ritterkreuz on 22 October 1940 after twenty victories. He amassed a score of thirty-six victories before dying from complications following the loss of a leg on the Eastern Front on 27 June 1941.

Middle: General Loerzer and Reichsmarschall Göring seem unhappy with the progress of the Battle.

Bottom: Major von Maltzahn, Kommodore of JG 53, with his Gruppe leaders and other successful pilots, taken early in 1941, after the Battle. Left to right: Schiess, Brändle, Wilcke, von Maltzahn, Bretnütz, Litjens, Brustellin, Erich Schmidt and Götz. The Bf 109E–4 behind them has the later type of spinner.

Top: From late summer 1940, the Bf 109 and 110 were used on a large scale as fighter-bombers. A Bf 109E–4/B is shown here.
Middle: A Bf 110 of ZG 26 receives its load of two 500kg. bombs.
Bottom: Bf 110E fighter-bombers; the 110E version appeared in spring 1941, but within the Battle of Britain period recognized by German historians.

The Channel Dash

Since the beginning of 1941, the battle cruisers *Scharnhorst* and *Gneisenau* and the heavy cruiser *Prinz Eugen* had lain at anchor in the French port of Brest, where their presence kept occupied not only part of the British Home Fleet, but also the Mediterranean Fleet which was stationed in the Gibraltar area. At this time, Hitler was fully involved with the preparations for the forthcoming campaign against the Soviet Union. Fearing a possible attack by a combined Soviet-British force, he ordered that his three cruisers be moved from Brest to Norwegian waters.

On 12 January 1942 a conference was held at Hitler's headquarters, the Wolfsschanze (Wolf's Lair) near Rastenburg in East Prussia, to organize this planned move, to be known as Operation Donnerkeil-Cerberus. As well as Hitler and Keitel there were present the Commander-in-Chief of the Navy, Admiral Raeder, battleship commanders Ciliax and Ruge, Chief of Air Staff Jeschonnek and fighter chief General Adolf Galland. They decided that the German cruisers should be moved by the shortest route, through the English Channel, in order to avoid contact with the British Home Fleet. All available fighter units of the Luftwaffe were to provide air cover for the flotilla.

Preparations began in utmost secrecy. General Martini, head of the German intelligence service, worked with his radar specialists to devise completely new decoy and jamming methods, while Navy minesweepers cleared the route. The Luftwaffe set up four fighter control-centres along the coast, and the following units were detailed to take part: JG 2 with three Gruppen, JG 26 with three Gruppen, JG 1 with two Gruppen, twelve aircraft from the Paris Fighter School and thirty Bf 110 night-fighters. In all, 282 fighter aircraft would be available for the 'umbrella'. At all times there would be at least sixteen, and occasionally thirty-two aircraft over the convoy.

The operation began on 11 February 1942. At 23.00 hours the big ships left Brest, escorted by seven destroyers. Early next morning, they were joined by a dozen torpedo-boats and day-fighters moved in to provide protection from above.

Drizzle concealed the flotilla until at noon they reached the narrowest part of the Channel at the Dover Straits, and were recognized by the British. Fifteen German Schnellboote (E-boats), which had arrived in the meantime, engaged attacking British surface craft. The first air combats began as six Swordfish torpedo-planes attacked and were shot down. British attacks continued through the day, and all were repulsed. At about 15.30 the flagship *Scharnhorst* struck a mine and stopped. British aircraft proceeded to attack her but were once again beaten off by fighters and anti-aircraft fire. At 16.05 *Scharnhorst* got under way again and followed the flotilla. At dusk, 19.30, the day-fighters were replaced by night-fighters. Apart from some slight mine damage, the operation had gone according to plan and was a great success. Cooperation between Navy and Luftwaffe had been exemplary. The British destroyer *Worcester* had been set alight, and seventy-one British aircraft had been shot down by fighters and ship-borne Flak. Germany had lost one patrol boat and seventeen aircraft.

For the British nation, the breakout – on their own 'doorstep' – came as a severe shock. The German flotilla proceeded on its course and reached its new anchorage in Norway on 13 February.

The battle cruisers break out. In tight formation and surrounded by destroyers and minesweepers, the big ships steam towards the Dover Straits.

Towards noon the weather deteriorates. Speed is increased, while fighters patrol constantly above the flotilla.

Around midday the ships are seen by the enemy and fired on by coastal batteries, the cruisers returning the fire. Attacks by British MTBs and Swordfish are beaten off by the fighters, Flak and light shipboard guns.

In the course of the day seventy-one British aircraft are brought down. Towards dusk the night-fighters take over the escort duties.

The operation has succeeded. Cooperation between Navy and Luftwaffe was exemplary.

The Mediterranean and North African Theatre

Following the loss of her colonies in East Africa, Italy was also in danger of being beaten in North Africa. Marshal Graziani's forces, which had advanced as far as Sidi Barrani, had been pushed back to Benghazi by the British. On 18 January 1941, at his mountain retreat at Berchtesgaden, Hitler promised Mussolini that he would send blocking forces under Panzergeneral Rommel to Tripoli. The first German soldiers landed on African soil on 11 February 1941 and, on 31 March, part of the Afrika Korps broke through between the widely separated British positions, and stormed eastwards as far as the Egyptian border, where the attack halted. Backup supplies were not forthcoming, as the British, operating from the island fortress of Malta, managed to inflict losses of 70 per cent on Axis convoys between Italy and Africa.

Between 20 May and 2 June 1941, the island of Crete was captured by German paratroops and airborne forces using 500 Ju 52 transports; but this important British base in the Mediterranean was occupied at a terrible cost in German lives and machines.

The Luftwaffe presence in North Africa was only small, and often short of fuel. It was unable to take an effective part in the fighting until Malta had been damaged and the supply lines re-established. In a big air offensive between 20 March and 28 April 1942, the German and Italian Air Forces attacked Malta's airfields and the harbour of La Valetta, rendering them unusable for some time. It would have now been logical to invade and occupy the island, but the means were lacking.

Meanwhile, the British managed to drive the German and Italian Armies back through Cyrenaica. Rommel counter-attacked with his second big offensive and drove the British back into Egypt. On 20/21 June 1942, the fortress of Tobruk fell into German hands after a bitter fight and, shortly after this success, Rommel was promoted to Generalfeldmarschall. However, the offensive petered out sixty miles from Alexandria. Malta was in use once again, and supplies to the Germany Army in North Africa were once more interrupted. A further air offensive against Malta failed to improve matters. Despite a courageous all-out effort, the Luftwaffe was thrown more and more onto the defensive. 23 October saw the beginning of the British counter-offensive at El Alamein, and by 4 October Rommel was forced to retreat.

On 18 November 1942, the Allies under General Eisenhower landed in Morocco and Algeria. German troops were now fighting on two fronts. Luftwaffe bomber Gruppen were sent to Tunisia and placed under the command of General Nehring. In December 1942, a stubborn air and tank battle raged in Algeria. This was the last chance for the Axis powers, but the final German attack, on 6 March 1943, was broken up by Allied bombing. On 12 May 1943 Generaloberst von Armin offered the capitulation of the Heeresgruppe Afrika, and 130,000 German soldiers marched into captivity.

Hundreds of Ju 52 transports ferry paratroops and Alpine troops to Crete.

Above: Bf 109E–4 of JG 77 on Crete, May 1941.

Above: Bf 109E–7s of 7./JG 26 on Sicily in spring 1941. At right, Leutnant Klaus Mietusch, Kapitän of 7. Staffel.

Right: Sicily, early 1941. Oberleutnant Joachim Müncheberg's Bf 109E–7 is prepared for a raid on Malta.
Below: Oberleutnant Joachim Müncheberg, who claimed three victories in one day, 1 May 1941.

Left: Leutnant Mietusch congratulates Müncheberg on another victory.
Below: MG 151 on a home-made anti-aircraft mounting with 5./JG 54.

Above: A Schwarm of Bf 109E–4s on a sweep.
Right: 16 May 1941. III./JG 77's Bf 109E–7s just before the Balkan campaign.
Bottom: Escorted by Bf 109E–4s of JG 27, Ju 87R Stukas head for Tobruk in summer 1941.

Top: Bf 109E–4s of III./JG 54 on an airfield in Rumania. The machine at left is brand new, and still bears its factory-applied radio-call-sign.

Middle: A few holes in Oberfähnrich Hans-Joachim Marseille's aircraft. Marseille's star was about to ascend.

Bottom: Gazala, June 1941. A Bf 109E–4 of 1./JG 27.

Top: The African adventure begins.

Middle: Hurricanes wrecked on the ground at Lamia in Greece.

Bottom: Dusty weather at I./JG 27's base at Gazala, June 1941. The aircraft in the foreground belongs to Oberleutnant Homuth.

A Rotte (two-plane formation) from I./JG 27 on a sweep over the desert. Note the temperate camouflage on the wingman's Bf 109E-4.

Right: Armourers of I./JG 27 loading 20mm. shells, summer 1941.

Below: An idyllic scene on a North African airfield. The wing of a derelict Caproni Ca 133 shades the tent which serves as a flight preparation room.

Left: Generalfeldmarschall Kesselring (left) talks to General der Panzertruppe (later Generalfeldmarschall) Rommel.
Below: Bf 109E–7 'Yellow 14' of 7./JG 26 in North Africa, summer 1941.

7./JG 26 at work and play, summer 1941. In the bottom photograph are left, Klaus Mietusch (with donkey) and third from left, Joachim Müncheberg.

Right: A distinguished visitor:
Generalfeldmarschall Kesselring addresses
the pilots of I./JG 27. Hans-Joachim
Marseille is seventh from the left.
Below: Left to right: Leutnant Stahlschmidt,
Hauptmann Gerlitz, Leutnant Marseille,
Hauptmann Neumann, Generalfeldmarschall
Kesselring and General Geissler.

Right: Hauptmann Edu Neumann, Kommandeur of I./JG 27, heaves himself out of his Bf 109.

Below: Hauptmann Edu Neumann presents yet another decoration to Marseille, autumn 1941.

Above: Martuba, February 1942. Oberleutnant Franzisket receives instructions from Hauptmann Homuth.
Below: A Stuka and artillery attack on a British armoured unit.

Above: The storm-cones are up. Bf 109F/Trop. on a desert airfield.
Below: Oberleutnant Franzisket, Adjutant of I./JG 27, keeps close contact with his charge, a Ju 87B of II./St.G.2. Fighter escort was essential for the vulnerable Stuka. Note the bomb crutch hanging down after release.

Right and below: Hungry mouths to feed at Martuba, February 1942. The aircraft are Bf 109F–2/Trop. of II./JG 27.

A spectacular prang at
Martuba. A Macchi Mc. 202 of
80 Squadriglia swerves into
parked aircraft. The pilot is
quickly rescued from his
burning machine.

Above: A Schwarm of Bf 109F–2/Trop. of I./JG 27.
Below: 21 February 1942: Leutnant Marseille pictured just after his forty-ninth and fiftieth victories. He was now top-scorer in Africa. The aircraft is a Bf 109F–2/Trop., 'Yellow 14'.

The new victories must be described and marked up, and the 109 made ready for her next sortie. In the photo at bottom left, Marseille is seen with Hptm. Homuth and other comrades.

Top: The command post of
I./JG 27 was 'Neumanns Bunte
Bühne' ('Neumann's colourful
stage'), a circus wagon
captured in France.
Middle: Scramble! A Schwarm
from I./JG 27 raises the dust at
Ain el Gazala.
Bottom: A Fieseler Storch
picks up the pilot of a bent Bf
109F–2/Trop. of JG 27.

Top: May 1942: Bf 109F–2/Trop. of III./JG 53.
Middle: Gazala airfield, home to various German and Italian wrecks and guarded here by a 2cm. Flak gun.
Bottom: Opening time at the 'Marabu' cinema, Martuba.

Top: Marseille and 'Yellow 14' return victorious yet again.
Middle: A Hurricane of 213 Squadron brought down by Marseille, February 1942.
Bottom: Oberfeldwebel Otto Schulz of II./JG 27 photographed a few days before his death, June 1942. Schulz failed to return from a sweep in the area of Sidi Rezegh on 17 June. His victory tally stood at fifty-one, of which forty-two were obtained in Africa.

Top left: Hauptmann Gustav Rödel, Kommandeur of II./JG 27 – one of the foremost of that unit's aces – pictured in summer 1942.
Top right and below: 10./JG 27 (top right) and 7./JG 27 (bottom) stationed in Sicily for fighter-bomber attacks on Malta, summer 1942.

Top: Happy pilots of Staffel Rollwage (5./JG 53) with a Bf 109 G–6/Trop., summer 1942. Such cheerful scenes were soon to become rare.

Middle: An air of expectancy at 5./JG 53.

Bottom: On 8 August 1942, Oberfeldwebel Rollwag chalks up his three hundredth sortie from Sicily. The rudder of his Bf 109G–6/Trop. shows thirty victories, but the third was not confirmed.

Hauptmann Hans-Joachim Marseille died in an accident on 30 September 1942. His Bf 109G–2 developed engine failure while returning from a mission. Marseille baled out over the German lines but struck the tailplane, and his parachute did not open. His death came as a shock not just to the Afrika-Jäger, but to the entire Luftwaffe. Marseille flew 382 missions and obtained 158 victories, 151 in Africa. He was buried in African soil, at Derna. The plaque below marks the site of his death.

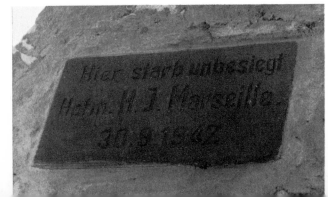

Left: Leutnant Armin Köhler, I./JG 77, with his Bf 109F–2 in North Africa, November 1942.
Below: Oberstleutnant Günther von Maltzahn of JG 53 in Tunisia describes his Geschwader's latest missions to a war reporter. The Italian unit is thought to be part of 51 Stormo.

Top: The end of a Bf 109E, probably belonging to III./JG 27.
Middle: Oberleutnant Schroer over the Aegean. The rudder of his Bf 109E—2/Trop. carries sixty victory bars.
Bottom left and right: Oberleutnant Werner Schroer, Staffelkapitän of 8./JG 27, at Kastelli, Crete, December 1942.

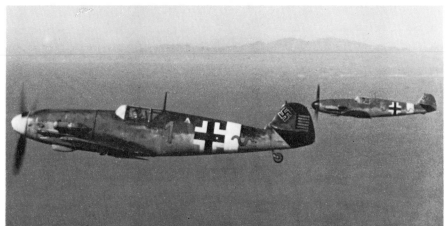

Top left: Generalfeldmarschall Rommel examines a crash-landed British Tomahawk.
Top right: Oberleutnant Dinger, Kapitän of 4./JG 53, with fifty-three victories in Tunisia, December 1942.
Middle: The Luftwaffe was being bombed out of Africa by the end of 1942.
Bottom: Major Heinz Bär awaits further events in Tunisia, early 1943.

Right: Major Bär talks with Kommodore Müncheberg. Third from left is Leutnant Köhler.
Below: Following a bombing raid in early 1943, II./JG 53's Tunisian airfield is repaired by an interesting vertical-boilered steam-roller. The aircraft to the right of the photograph is a Bf 109G–2.

Left: Hauptmann Bühligen of II./JG 2 amassed forty victories in Tunisia.
Below: A Bf 109G–6/R6 of JG 53 in a Splitter-box, or blast pen, Sicily, summer 1943.

Above, left and right: Major Joachim Müncheberg, Kommodore of JG 77 since 1 October 1942, fell in action on 23 March 1943, when the wings came off his aircraft. Müncheberg's victories totalled 135. He was buried at El Aonnia and later moved to the Heroes' Cemetery at Les Massem near Tunis.
Middle: An Airacobra shot down over Tunisia.
Bottom: An interesting view of the 'innards' of a Bf 109F–2/Trop.

Top: An armourer of I./JG 77 at work, summer 1943 in Southern Italy.
Middle: Leutnant Reinert, of II./JG 77, in Sicily, early 1943. Reinert was awarded the Oak Leaves on 6 October 1942 after 103 victories. By the end of the war, his total had risen to 174.
Bottom: A Schwarm of Bf 109G–6s of JG 53 in Sicily.

Above: A visit from top brass from Berlin, May 1943. The pilots seem sceptical about the possibility of holding Sicily. Left to right: Generalmajor Osterkamp (with the white cap), General Wolfram von Richthofen, Lützow, Steinhoff and Wilcke.

Right: In May and June 1943, the German fighter airfields in Sicily were heavily bombed by the U.S.A.F.

Top: Three JG 53 aces in Catania, June 1943. Left to right: Leutnant Broennle, Hauptmann 'Tutti' Müller and Oberleutnant Dinger.
Middle: An Me 323 'Gigant' flies supplies into Sicily. In the foreground there is a Bf 109G–6/R6 of JG 53.
Bottom: Pilots of II./JG 53 in Sicily, summer 1943. Left to right: Ehrenberger, Lindes, Dinger, Michalski and Hammer.

Above: Somewhere in Italy, summer 1943, IV./JG 27's 109G–6s await their next mission. Note the absence of unit and personal markings, possibly an indication that the Gruppe was constantly in action against the enemy.
Below left: Hauptmann Gerhard Michalski with pilots of his Gruppe, II./JG 53 in Italy. Third from left is Oberfeldwebel Rollwage, leader of 5. Staffel, and at right, next to Michalski, is Oberfeldwebel Ehrenburger.
Below right: General Galland and Oberstleutnant Lützow in Southern Italy, summer 1943.

IV./JG 3's rocket-armed Bf 109G–6/R2s came to Italy to intercept the American bomber formations.

Above: Machines of IV./JG 27 return to Kalamaki, near Athens, after a combat with P-38 Lightnings, 17 November 1943.
Right: Oberfeldwebel Heinrich Bartels brought down his seventieth opponent during the above action.

Top: Coffee time for Major Rödel, Kommodore of JG 27 in Greece (probably at Kalamaki).
Middle: A Bf 109G–6/R6 of I./JG 27 on escort duty in Southern France.
Bottom: Hauptmann Jürgen Harder took his I./JG 53 to Rumania in early summer 1944. By this time Germany was hard pressed on all fronts, and Luftwaffe units were heavily outnumbered.

The Soviet Campaign

The invasion of the Soviet Union began at 3.15 a.m. on 22 June 1941 with a mighty artillery barrage. Germany had opened a second front and thereby sealed her military doom. Along this front, extending for nearly 1,400 kilometres (870 miles) from the Baltic to the Black Sea, three German army groups, supported by 1,300 aircraft, thrust into Russia's vast open countryside. In surprise attacks, German bombers dived on crowded Russian airfields, destroying most of the parked aircraft and preparing the way for a headlong advance by the army. The Luftwaffe's balance sheet for the first day of the offensive read as follows: 322 Soviet aircraft shot down by fighters and Flak, and 1,489 wrecked on the ground. However, despite the tremendous losses inflicted upon the Russians, the Luftwaffe was unable to eliminate the Soviet Air Force. In 1941, Soviet aircraft production increased four-fold and a total of 15,735 aircraft of all types were delivered to the military during the year. This Germany could not prevent, lacking the long-range bombers necessary to destroy the distant production centres for these Soviet aircraft. Although German fighter victories rose by leaps and bounds, the Soviets kept pouring more and more machines into the conflict. At the same time, Soviet armies were being encircled and wiped out in huge Kesselschlachten, or 'cauldron battles'.

The German offensive was halted outside Moscow by the onset of the Russian winter, and, on 6 December, a Soviet counter-offensive began forcing the Germans to fall back. From August 1941, Allied convoys had been bringing war materials along the Arctic route to Murmansk; while German aircraft and U-boats were to some degree successful against these convoys, they could not stem the flow.

In the winter of 1941/42, four Soviet armies broke through the German lines between Army Groups North and Centre, and surrounded X and part of XI Army Corps around Demyansk, and a further 3,500 men of the 281st Infantry Division at Kholm. For a year and eighteen days the Luftwaffe kept the 100,000 men in the Demyansk 'cauldron' supplied by means of a 250-kilometre (150-mile) air bridge, until they were relieved by a counter-offensive. An airlift to Kholm was similarly successful.

In the summer of 1942, the German armies were once more on the advance, over the Don and the Volga and on towards the Caucasus mountains. The Luftwaffe was increasingly called upon for close-support duties for the ground fighting, but the great depth of the penetration, 1,000 kilometres (600 miles), caused supply difficulties, so that ever fewer aircraft were serviceable.

The onset of the second winter of the campaign made the immense front, stretching from Lake Ladoga to the Black Sea, untenable. The southern sector was forced to withdraw and, by the end of November 1942, Sixth Army, under General Paulus, was surrounded in Stalingrad. The Luftwaffe was again given the job of flying supplies into the 'cauldron'. The long-term support, from the air, of a whole army of 250,000 men was impossible considering the capacity of the transport aircraft available. Bad weather and ever-lengthening flying distances made a catastrophe inevitable, but nevertheless supplies were flown into the city until it was overrun. The last radio message out of Stalingrad, on 2 February 1943, was: 'We have done our duty down to the last man ...'.

Hard fighting throughout the winter regained for the Soviets the territory lost in the 1942 summer offensive, and the front finally stabilized again in April 1943, the German Orel salient, pointing east, the Soviet Kursk salient pointing west. The Germans now planned a pincer-movement, to be known as Unternehmen Zitadelle (Operation 'Citadel'), to enclose the Soviet armies; but the Soviets knew the date and time of the German attack. Hundreds of Soviet aircraft descended on the packed German airfields, but fighters of JG 52 and JG 3 were able to get airborne at the last minute and intercepted the raid. In one of the biggest air battles of the Soviet Campaign, 120 attacking Soviet aircraft were shot down in rapid succession. The thinned-out Soviet formations were unable to bomb accurately, owing to Flak, and the raid produced little success. German troops made deep inroads into the Soviet front, but the operation failed for lack of reserves. On 11 July, the Soviets returned to the attack with overwhelming force: Army and Luftwaffe units were needed to protect the flanks and cover gaps in the front line, and the Germans were forced back on the defensive. Local successes could not hide the truth; the Eastern Front was falling back, and the retreat, once begun, could not be stopped.

Above: Hauptmann Hrabak and Oberleutnant Philipp watch the fuelling of a Bf 109E of the Stab (Staff) flight, II./JG 54, shortly before the Eastern campaign.
Below: 5./JG 54 equipped with Bf 109E–4s at Deta, near Arad, April 1941.

Above: 7./JG 52, early 1941. Identified pilots are, front row centre:
Zwernemann, far right: Rossmann, second row left: Dammers, and top:
Grislawski.

Above: Artist's impression of a fighter strike on a Russian airfield, end of June
1941.

Above: An M–103-engined SB-2 destroyed on the ground.

Above: I-16s and I-153s were wrecked in thousands on the ground by the Luftwaffe's first heavy attacks, summer 1941.

Left: Heinz Bär sends an SB-2 down in flames.
Below: Oberleutnant Heinz Bär as Staffelkapitän of 12./JG 51 in Russia, July 1941.

Right: Major Walter Oesau, Kommandeur of III./JG 3, with
General von Greim, July 1941.
Bottom: A combat with 'Ratas' as imagined by a war artist.
His knowledge of front-line German aircraft seems to have
been a bit out-of-date!

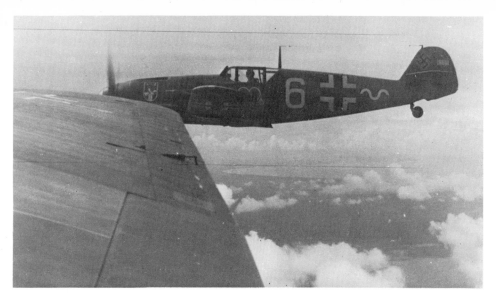

Above: Eight victory bars decorate the rudder of this Bf 109G—2 of 7./JG 54, seen here over the Russian plains in summer 1941.

Below: Fürst (Prince) Wilcke, Kommandeur of III./JG 53 in summer 1941.

Right: Bf 109 G-2s of 7./JG 54 about to take off.

Bottom left: Hauptmann Wilck's conversation with one of his Gruppe is recorded for posterity. Behind Wilcke, half-hidden, is 'Tutti' Müller.

Bottom right: Generalfeldmarschall Kesselring visits III./JG 53.

Above: Ritterkreuze for Leutnant Schramm (right) after twenty-four victories, and Hauptmann Wilcke after twenty-five victories, 9 August 1941, near Surash. On the left is Leutnant Schmidt and next to him is Generalfeldmarschall Kesselring.

Right: Leutnant Erich Schmidt, III./JG 53, at Dubno after his forty-fourth victory on 27 August 1941. Leutnant Schmidt went missing after being shot down by anti-aircraft fire on 31 August 1941, by which time he had forty-seven victories to his credit.

Above left: Hauptmann Franz von Werra as commanding officer of I./JG 53 in Russia, summer 1941, after his legendary escape from British captivity. On 25 October 1941 he was drowned when his aircraft suffered engine failure and plunged into the sea near Vlissingen. Von Werra's victory tally of twenty-one included thirteen obtained in Russia.

Above right: Oberleutnant 'Hubs' Mütherich, Kapitän of 5./JG 54, was killed in a landing accident on 9 September 1941, with a score of forth-three victories.

Below: A Bf 109 of II./JG 54 burns out after a forced landing, summer 1941.

Above: No more flying for this I-16 Rata.
Below: Leutnant Ostermann, Kapitän of 7./JG 54, sets out on one of his far-ranging patrols, end of October 1941.

Left: Arming Ostermann's aircraft, October 1941.
Right: Applying victory bar number thirty-seven: Ostermann received the Ritterkreuz on 4 September 1941 after twenty-nine victories, and reached one hundred and two before being shot down near Amossovo by nine Soviet fighters on 9 August 1942.

Top: Inside a mobile workshop.

Middle: Oberstleutnant Werner Mölders visits II./JG 51 a few weeks before his death. On 22 November 1941 Mölders lost his life in an air crash while on his way to attend Udet's funeral. In 300 operational flights, Mölders notched-up one hundred and fifteen victories: fourteen in Spain, sixty-eight in the West and thirty-three in Russia.

Bottom: The State funeral of Generalluftzeugmeister (General in charge of aircraft production) Ernst Udet on 22 November 1941. Udet shot himself in a fit of depression.

The funeral of Oberst Mölders in Berlin, 28 November 1941. To the right of Göring, in the centre picture, are fighter aces Schalk and Lützow. In the bottom picture, taken at the Invalidenfriedhof, fighter pilots Schnell, Priller, Hahn and Streib form the front rank of the cortège.

Top: A wrecked Soviet aircraft and a Bf 109F–4 of JG 54 on a Russian airfield.

Middle: Bf 109F of I./JG 54, winter 1941–42.

Bottom: The newly-appointed General der Jagdflieger (General of the Fighter Arm), Adolf Galland, at Ryelbitzy. Left to right: Doktor Vogel, Major Andres, Major Janke, Oberstleutnant Trautloft, Oberst Galland, Hauptmann Hrabak, Hauptmann Brustellin and Oberleutnant Wendl, winter 1941–42.

Above and below: In February 1942, I./JG 51 was flying escort for Ju 52 transports, supplying the Demyansk Cauldron. Often only one Rotte (pair) of fighters was available to protect 150 Ju 52s.

Telephoto shots of an air combat in which a Soviet Il–2 pilot meets his match, February 1942.

Above: Bf 109F–4 of 6./JG 5 on a sweep near Petsamo, spring 1942.
Left: Leutnant Heinrich Ehrler, 6./JG 5, in May 1942 after thirty-two victories.

Above: Leutnant Ehrler and Hauptmann Carganico bask in the spring sunshine at Petsamo, around May 1942. Ehrler's tally-stick shows thirty-four victories.
Right: Oberfeldwebel Franz-Josef Beerenbrock of IV./JG 51 had notched-up sixty-two victories by spring 1942.

Above left and right: Feldwebel 'Peppi' Jennewein, world ski champion of 1939, was with I./JG 51 at Orel. He went missing with a score of eighty-six on 26 July 1943.

Left: Hauptmann 'Gaudi' Krafft, Kommandeur of I./JG 51 near Orel in spring 1942. Krafft was shot down by anti-aircraft guns near Bjelic on 14 December 1942 and killed by Soviet troops.

Top: Oberleutnant Adolf Dickfeld of III./JG 52, shot down nine opponents on 14 May 1942, to bring his score to ninety. By the end of the war it had reached 136, 115 of which were achieved in the East.

Middle: Hauptmann Reinhard Seiler, Kommandeur of III./JG 54, with his Bf 109F–4. 'Seppl' Seiler was wounded and invalided home in July 1943, but returned to take command of JG 54 in August 1944. His score finally reached 109.

Bottom: Evening on an eastern airfield, May 1942. The last fighters are coming home to roost. Who is missing?

Left: One more victory for Leutnant Hans Beisswenger, Kapitän of 6./JG 54. This pilot, who received the Ritterkreuz for his forty-seventh victory in May 1942, and the Eichenlaub (Oak Leaves) for his hundredth in September, attained a score of 152 before he went missing on 6 March 1943 in combat with ten Soviet fighters.

Below: General Förster awards the Ritterkreuz to Leutnants Beisswenger and Hannig, 9 May 1942. Hannig, whose score then stood at forty-eight, became commanding officer of 2./JG 2 on the English Channel early in 1943, and achieved ninety-eight victories before falling to Spitfires near Caen on 15 May 1943.

Top: 5./JG 54's captured MiG-3.
Middle: A Soviet SB-2 bomber after a forced landing.
Bottom: Hauptmann Carganico, Kommandeur of II./JG 5, salutes Feldwebel Rudi Müller of 6./JG 5 on the award of his Ritterkreuz for forty-one victories, 19 June 1942.

Left: Oberfeldwebel Max Stotz of II./JG 54 sports his new Ritterkreuz, 19 June 1942. Stotz was to win 189 air combats before he disappeared near Vitebsk on 19 August 1943.

Below: Oberfeldwebel Josef Zwernemann of II./JG 52, newly decorated on 23 June 1942. The Ritterkreuz was awarded after his fifty-seventh victory, the Oak Leaves on 31 October 1942 after 101. 'Jupp' was shot down and killed by a Mustang near Gardelegen on 8 April 1944, while serving as Kapitän of 1./JG 11. His score then stood at 126.

Above: Oberleutnant Helmut Mertens, of I./JG 3, after his fiftieth victory, September 1942.
Right: Leutnant Hans Fuss, Staffelkapitän of 6./JG 3, 22 July 1942. His score so far was sixty-seven.

Top: Ninety-five bars for Hauptmann Kurt Brändle, Kommandeur of II./JG 3, at Frolow outside Stalingrad, August 1942.
Middle: 8./JG 52's aces, September 1942. Unteroffizier Gratz, Oberleutnant Rall, Feldwebel Dammers.
Bottom: Bf 109F escorting Stukas over the southern sector of the Eastern Front.

Right: Hauptmann Johannes Steinhoff, Kommandeur of II./JG 52, notched up his hundredth victory on 31 August 1942. His final score of 176 (of which 148 were achieved in the East), included four heavy bombers; he claimed six victories while flying the Me 262 with JG 7. Steinhoff was severely injured in a take-off accident on 18 April 1945.
Below: Stuka escort: a Bf 109F–4 of I./JG 51.

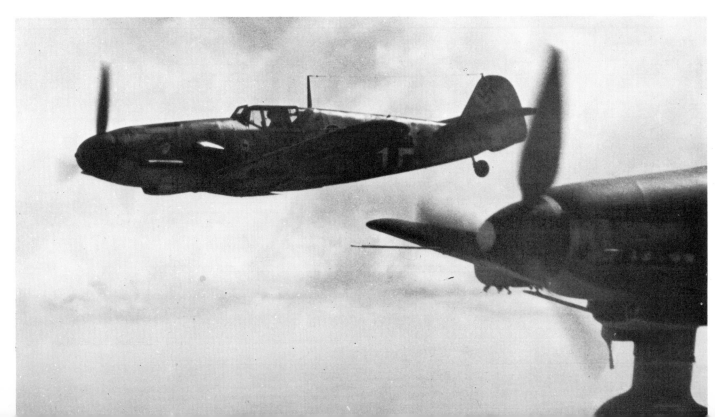

Above left: Hauptmann Leppla, Kommandeur of III./JG 51, summer 1942.
Above right: Unteroffizier Oskar Romm of I./JG 51 converts to the Fw 190 at Königsberg.
Left: Hauptmann Grasser, Kommandeur of II./JG 51, and Hauptmann Leppla of III./JG 51, summer 1942.

Right: A Spanish pilot of 15./JG 51 in his Fw 190A–5.
Below: This Bf 109E–4 of JG 51 caught fire during a belly-landing in summer 1942.

Above right: The Kommodore of JG 77, Major Gordon Gollob, writes up his diary outside Stalingrad.
Above left and bottom: Major Gollob ends the war for the pilot of an Il-2.

Above: Interrogating the much-decorated Russian pilot after his capture. Known pilots are: second from the left, Dickfeld, and next to him, Gollob.
Right and opposite page, Top: Oberst Günther Lützow takes his leave of JG 3 in southern Russia, summer 1942 and hands over to Hauptmann Wilcke.

Below: A peaceful scene: A 2cm. Vierlingsflak (Quad anti-aircraft gun) guards an airfield in the southern sector.

Above and below: A sudden attack by Il-2s causes spectacular devastation.

Leutnant Hans-Joachim Heyer notched up JG 54's three thousandth victory on 4 November 1942. Heyer, with a score of fifty-three, was killed five days later in a collision with a Soviet fighter.

Hannes Trautloft, Kommodore of JG 54.

Top: Kommodore Hannes Trautloft of the Grünherz (Green Heart) Geschwader with his Kommandeure: Seiler, Hrabak and Philipp.
Middle: Oberstleutnant Graf visits his old unit, III./JG 52 at the end of September 1942. He is seen here with Hauptmann Rall and Hauptmann Wiese.
Bottom: Hermann Graf surrounded by his trusty Oberfeldwebeln. From left to right: Zwernemann, Steffen, Graf, Rossmann, Grotz and Süss.

Top: Bf 109F–4s of 7./JG 54 at Siverskaya, around December 1942.
Middle: Leutnant Max Stotz of II./JG 54 with a Bf 109F, on Lake Ilmen, winter 1942–43.
Bottom: Hannes Trautloft in his Bf 109F on Lake Ilmen, winter 1942–43.

Fw 190s of I./JG 54, winter 1942–43. The machine in the top photograph is that of Hauptmann Hans Philipp, the Gruppenkommandeur.

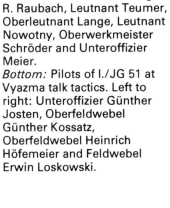

Top: One horse-power transport in use with I./JG 54. Ground crews maintained serviceability in almost impossible conditions during the winter of 1942–43.
Middle: A civilized meal in the Kasino (Pilots' Mess) at Gatschina Castle. Left to right: R. Raubach, Leutnant Teumer, Oberleutnant Lange, Leutnant Nowotny, Oberwerkmeister Schröder and Unteroffizier Meier.
Bottom: Pilots of I./JG 51 at Vyazma talk tactics. Left to right: Unteroffizier Günther Josten, Oberfeldwebel Günther Kossatz, Oberfeldwebel Heinrich Höfemeier and Feldwebel Erwin Loskowski.

Right: A Bf 109G–6 drones serenely over the snowfields of northern Russia.
Below: I./JG 51's Fw 190A–3s were based on the frozen Lake Ivan near Velikye Luki in January 1943.

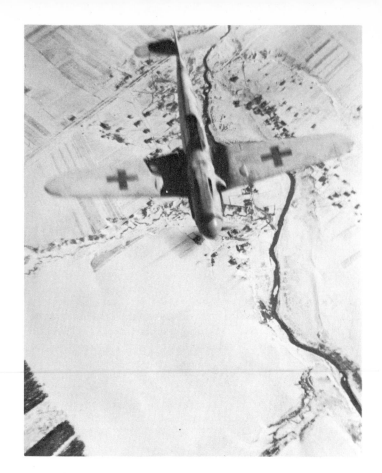

Bf 109Fs of JG 5 escort a flight of Ju 87D Stukas over the Polar Sea.

Right: The Bf 109E–4 of Hauptmann Günther Scholz, Kommandeur of III./JG 5, northern Finland, spring 1943.

Middle: 6./JG 5 in the far north, spring 1943. Front row from left to right: Feldwebel Döbrich, unknown, Oberleutnant Ehrler, Oberfeldwebel Müller, Unteroffizier Mörs, Oberleutnant Weissenberger, and seated at back: Oberfeldwebel Brunner, unknown.

Bottom: 'Bubi' Hartmann added a U-2 to his score on 15 May 1943.

Leutnant 'Jupp' Zwernemann did not need to ask permission to celebrate Hauptmann Rall's latest victory, spring 1943.

Above left: Leutnant Walter Nowotny about to take off.
Above right: The Stukas have called for an escort.
Below: Was the joke printable? Major Hubertus von Bonin, Kommandeur of III./JG 54, and Leutnant Walter Nowotny, Kapitän of 1./JG 54.

Above left and right: Hauptmann Johannes Wiese of I./JG 52 with something to smile about – one hundred victories under his hat (around 10 July 1943).
Below: A hot summer's day.

Top: War photographers on the Eastern Front did not often have either time or inclination to record such scenes as this. Both A hot summer's day and this picture, After sunset, have a unique beauty. The Bf 109G–6s belong to 2./JG 52, led at the time by Hauptmann Wiese.

Middle: Hauptmann Günther Rall, Kommandeur of III./JG 52, with his ground crew on the occasion of his 200th victory, 29 August 1943. The scene is Makeyevka airfield.

Bottom: Something to celebrate too at 6./JG 5's base in the north. Feldwebel Hans Döbrich receives the Ritterkreuz on 19 September 1943 after fifty-two victories. Left to right: Hauptmann Ehrler, Feldwebel Döbrich, and Major Scholz, the commanding officer.

Above: Two Kommandeure of JG 54, autumn 1943 in Russia: Hauptmann Rudorffer (II. Gruppe) and Hauptmann Ademeit (I. Gruppe).

Below: On 2 October 1943, Leutnant Erich Hartmann of 9./JG 52 vanquished his 121st opponent, a LaGG-5, while flying this Bf 109G–6 over Novosaporovyi.

Above: Oberfeldwebel Otto Kittel receives his Ritterkreuz from Hauptmann Nowotny on 29 October 1943. Between them, these two pilots amassed 525 aerial victories.
Below: A coffee and cakes celebration for Otto Kittel. On the left is Hauptmann Nowotny, and on the right is Major von Bonin.

Above left: Fan mail for Walter Nowotny and 'Quax' Schnörrer.
Above right: Oberfeldwebel Toni Döbele and the standard of 1./JG 54.
Below: Rudi Rademacher, then of E-Gruppe Ost (Replenishment Gruppe East) at Sagan, has just received the Ritterkreuz from Oberst Trautloft, Kommodore of JG 54, 30 August 1944.

Meinem lieben Quax
zur Erinnerung an die
vielen preußigen und
lustigen Situationen,
die wir zusammen in
diesem gewaltigen Kriege
gemeistert haben und
noch meistern werden.
Von Dank will ich nicht
reden.
Bleib ein anständiger
Kerl.
Dein Nowi

Real team-mates: the Kommandeur and his wingman. On 12 November 1943, Karl Schnörrer was forced to abandon his burning aircraft at an altitude of 70 metres (230 feet), and was severely injured. Nowotny personally took his friend to hospital. 'Quax' kept the above portrait and letter of thanks and encouragement at his bedside until he recovered. Schnörrer was later to witness Nowotny's fatal crash in an Me 262.

Hauptmann Walter Nowotny takes off in his Fw 190A. His eventual tally was 258 victories. In February 1944, he took command of Schulgeschwader (Training Geschwader) 101. At the beginning of July, he was nominated leader of the famous 'Erprobungskommandos Nowotny', equipped with the world's first jet fighter, the Me 262. On 8 November 1944, after shooting down a four-engined bomber, he suffered an engine failure and was attacked by the escorting Mustangs. He was killed in the ensuing crash.

Above left: The crew chief helps Nowotny on with his parachute.
Above right: Two Schwärme of Focke-Wulfs drop in to their home field.
Left and below: Oberfeldwebel Albin Wolf of 6./JG 54, and his Fw 190A–5. His 135th victory was also JG 54's 7,000th. He fell to anti-aircraft fire on 2 April 1944.

Top: Fighter escort, 1943–44. Stukas had a hard time attacking Soviet tank formations, and the German fighters were heavily outnumbered.
Middle: The pilot of this badly damaged Fw 190A–4 has not yet left the cockpit after his crash-landing, February 1944.
Bottom: Among recipients of the Eichenlaub (Oak Leaves) on 2 March 1944, are Seiler, Ademeit, Krupinski and 'Bubi' Hartmann.

Top: Here's to Hauptmann Gerhard Barkhorn's 250th victory.
Middle: Barkhorn, Kommandeur of II./JG 52, 13 February 1944.
Bottom: Oberfeldwebel Günther Josten, one of the up-and-coming aces. In 1944 he flew with 3./JG 51, and obtained 178 victories by the war's end.

Above: Oberstleutnant Trautloft visits I./JG 51. Known pilots are Trautloft (second from left), Josten (third from left), and Romm (fourth from left).

Left: Oberleutnant Erich Hartmann and his crew chief Heinz Mertens, 24 August 1944.

Top: Unteroffizier Jünger and a radio operator listen intently to the pilots.
Middle: A wild greeting as Hartmann 'buzzes' the airfield.
Bottom: The amateur photographer who took this picture, moved the camera in his excitement. Eleven victories on 24 August 1944 brought Hartmann's score to 301. The sash was made of toilet paper.

Above left: Hauptmann Horst Ademeit, Kommandeur of I./JG 54, went missing across the Russian lines near Dünaburg on 8 August 1944, brought down by infantry fire. His victory tally then stood at 166.

Above right: Major Erich Rudorffer, Kommandeur of II./JG 54, in Kurland. Rudorffer was awarded the Oak Leaves on 11 April 1944 after 130 victories, the Swords on 25 January 1945 after 210 victories, and finished the war with 222 victories as Commanding Officer of the Me 262-equipped II./JG 7.

Leutnant Anton Hafner, Staffelkapitän of 8./JG 51, received the Oak Leaves on 11 April 1944 after 134 victories. He reached 204 victories before colliding with a tree while pursuing a Yak-9 on 17 June 1944.

Top: Leutnant Hafner in his Bf 109G–6 in Russia, summer 1944.
Middle: An unwelcome visitor: a heavily armoured Il-2 has just dropped its bombs.
Bottom: This two-seater Il-2 was written-off in Rumania, summer 1944.

Above: Obleser, Gratz and Hartmann show a touching concern for their Kommodore, Oberstleutnant Dietrich Hrabak.
Right: A successful team: Oberleutnant Hartmann and his faithful crew chief, Heinz Mertens, 25 September 1944.

653 victories together: Erich Hartmann and Gerhard Barkhorn in Hungary, 1944.

The Defence of the Reich

The relatively heavy losses sustained by the R.A.F. in their daylight raids on the German Bight forced the British to go over to night operations against the Reich. However, up to October 1942, forty-five daylight raids were flown by small formations. Since the beginning of the Russian campaign, the major part of the Luftwaffe's fighting in the west had been performed by JG 2, JG 26 and, from the end of 1940, by JG 1, which was then in process of formation. In February 1942, Air Marshal Sir Arthur Harris took control of Allied Bomber Command, and a substantial increase in day and night raids followed. On 17 April 1942, British bombers made a daylight attack upon the MAN factory at Augsburg. The first of the 1,000-bomber raids against a single city, Cologne, took place on the night of 30/31 May 1942. The B-17 Flying Fortresses of the U.S. Eighth Air Force, which had begun arriving in Scotland at the beginning of July, supported the Allied landings in North Africa, contributing materially to their success. On 27 January 1943, the town of Wilhelmshaven became the Americans' first target in Germany. Long-range P-38 Lightnings flew fighter escort, but proved inferior to the German Bf 109 and Fw 190 fighters.

In April 1943, pilots were transferred from JG 1 to form the nucleus of a new Geschwader, JG 11, for service in the west. From now on, the three Gruppen of this Geschwader were at the focus of the defensive action. On 17 April, the Americans carried out a heavy attack on Bremen – one of the Allied raids, occurring round the clock, that now forced the German High Command to concentrate more fighters in the Reich. Jagdgruppen were brought home from Russia, Italy and the Mediterranean and sent into action against the bomber streams. Overwhelmingly outnumbered, they sustained ever-rising losses. The great hope of the German pilots, the arrival in service of the Me 262, the world's first operational jet fighter, was delayed by more than a year because Hitler had demanded that this machine be converted into a fast bomber. Many nightfighters and Zerstörer (Bf 110s) were lost while engaged in rocket attacks on American four-engined day-bombers. However, after the death of Ernst Udet, with aircraft production now in the hands of Generalluftzeugmeister Milch and Reichsminister Speer, General Galland's wish for more fighter aircraft was fulfilled. Nevertheless, priority was still given to front-line units abroad.

On 17 August 1943, the Americans mounted a double raid on Schweinfurt and Regensburg, but the German defences accounted for sixty bombers shot down and over one hundred badly damaged. From 8 to 14 October, America lost a further 148 machines in attacks on German armament production centres. However, the favourable situation for Germany was reversed when, at the beginning of 1944, the new long-range P-51 Mustang escort fighter appeared in service. It now became very difficult for German pilots to intercept the bombers.

Hitler persisted in his refusal to release the Me 262 for use as a fighter. Not until 1944, when the Allies landed in France and the outnumbered fighter Geschwader were weakening, did he relent. On 7 July 1944, a new unit proved itself in battle over Oschersleben. This was Major Dahl's special purpose Geschwader, the Rammjäger (Ram-Fighters), and they brought down over thirty four-engined bombers with attacks pressed home even to the point of collision. Still the war nibbled remorselessly away at the substance of the Sturmjäger (home defence fighter arm). All hope now lay with the Me 262. The Erprobungskommando (Test Command) at Lechfeld, under Major Nowotny, was able to assemble initial experience with the aircraft. After Nowotny's death, JG 7 was founded under the command of Oberstleutnant Steinhoff, and was equipped with Me 262s. Meanwhile, in Jagdverband (Fighter Unit) 44, General Galland brought together experienced aces from all the Geschwader, but the time for great pilots was past. Enemy fighters lay in wait around airfields, pouncing on the heavily outnumbered jets as they took off and landed.

The fronts were collapsing inwards; the western Allies were at the Rhine, the Russians outside Berlin, towns in Germany lay in ruins and Italy was being lost piecemeal. In the face of insuperable difficulties, the German fighter arm had more than done its duty. 150,000 German airmen had fallen, including 70,000 pilots. This is a figure that should never be forgotten.

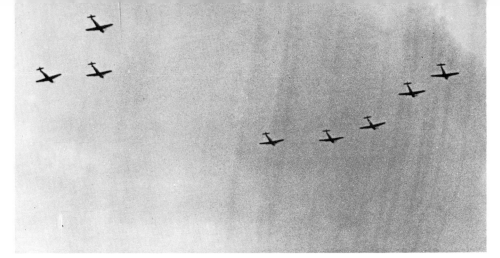

Top: A returning Schwarm of Bf 109Fs.

Middle: Hauptmann Egon Mayer as Staffelkapitän of 7./JG 2 in his Bf 109F. He was the first pilot on the Channel front to chalk-up 100 victories.

Bottom: 6. Staffel, JG 2 under Oberleutnant Rudorffer in the process of re-equipping with the Fw 190A–2, May 1942.

Left: Major Walter Oesau took over as Kommodore of JG 2 in August 1941. This Geschwader bore the brunt of the action in the west. Oesau shot down his 100th opponent on 26 October 1941.

Below: The famous British fighter ace, Group Captain Douglas Bader, who flew with two artificial legs, was shot down on 9 August 1941 by a pilot of JG 26. Here he is entertained by Kommodore Adolf Galland.

Above: A military funeral for a fallen British airman.

Below: Squadron Leader Bob Stanford Tuck was shot down in this Spitfire on 28 January 1942. He was brought down during a ground attack and captured, ending his run of twenty-nine victories.

Right: A toast to JG 2's 1,000th victory at Beaumont-le-Roger, 17 April 1942.
Below left: Jagdführer 3 (Fighter Commander 3), Oberst Max Ibel, visits Major Oesau's JG 2 'Richthofen' at Beaumont-le-Roger, 29 April 1942.
Below right: II./JG 2 got the new Focke-Wulf on 18 May 1942.

Above: Oberleutnant Frank Liesendahl's Bf 109F–4. Liesendahl, the commanding officer of 10./JG 2, led his Staffel with great success in Jabo (fighter-bomber) attacks on Channel shipping until he was posted missing on 17 July 1942.
Below left: Hauptmann Müncheberg, Kommandeur II./JG 26, summer 1942.
Below right: I./JG 26's mascot greets the commanding officer, Hauptmann Johannes Seifert, on his return from a successful sortie. The aeroplane is an Fw 190A–4.

Above: Two Channel aces, Egon Mayer and Joachim Müncheberg, talking shop.
Below: III./JG 26 about to set off from Wevelghem, 1 June 1942. In the background is Hauptmann Priller's Fw 190A–3.

A Fw 190A—4 of JG 2 taxies out. Overhead, a dogfight is already raging.

Above left: Oberleutnant Rudolf Pflanz, a highly successful Channel pilot, was killed in combat with Spitfires near Abbeville on 31 July 1942.

Above right: Oberfeldwebel Josef Wurmheller (right) and Major Walter Oesau in the summer of 1942. Wurmheller was one of the top fighter pilots on the Channel coast.

Below: 8./JG 2 in northern France. The nearest machine is Wurmheller's.

Left: Oberfeldwebel Josef Wurmheller recounts his latest victory.
Below: Pilots of III./JG 2 in the summer of 1942. Wurmheller is nearest the camera, Pflanz is second from the right.

Above: Fw 190A–2s of 7./JG 2 at Théville in readiness.
Below left: Hauptmann 'Assi' Hahn of III./JG 2, after his sixty-second victory, early July 1942.
Below right: Egon Mayer and other pilots of III./JG 2 at readiness.

Top: Oberleutnant Siegfried Schnell with pilots of his 9./JG 2 on the Channel coast.
Middle: 'Assi' Hahn and Siegfried Schnell, autumn 1942.
Bottom: The waiting game for 9./JG 2 in southern France, November 1942. The aircraft are Fw 190A–3s.

Final assembly and roll-out of Bf 109G–6s. The aircraft at bottom are fitted with sand filters for tropical use.

Top: The appealing lines of the Messerschmitt are readily apparent in this picture of a Bf 109G–6/R6, fitted with MG 151 gun pods.
Middle: With flaps fully lowered, an Fw 190A–6 sweeps-in to land.
Bottom: A written-off Fw 190, 9 October 1942.

Top: Alongside the Spitfire and Mustang, the P-47 Thunderbolt was a tough opponent for the Luftwaffe's fighters. This one fell into German hands after a forced landing.

Middle: When Oberstleutnant Hermann Graf took over JG 50 in May 1943, he brought some aces with him from the Karaja-Staffel, 9./JG 52. From left: Grislawski, Graf, Füllgrabe and Süss.

Bottom: Hauptmann 'Wutz' Galland, Kommandeur of II./JG 26, with Oberleutnant Ebersberger, the end of May 1943. On 17 August 1943, Galland was shot down by Thunderbolts and killed, while attacking a bomber.

Top: In memory of their late Kapitän, H.-J. Marseille, 3./JG 27 carried this modified badge for a time.

Middle: Oberst Walter Oesau, Kommodore of JG 2, in his Fw 190A–4. In the background are the Staffel's Bf 109s.

Bottom: 1./JG 2, a high-altitude Staffel, in the west, summer 1943.

A take-off of the prototype Schwalbe (Swallow), the Me 262 V3, in 1942. The remark of Adolf Galland, on flying this aircraft in May 1943, that 'it was as if an angel were pushing,' has gone down in aeronautical history. Note the tailwheel configuration of the prototype; production 262s had a nosewheel.

Another bold enterprise was the Me 163 (Komet), powered by a liquid-fuelled rocket engine. Several experienced young pilots lost their lives testing this aircraft at Bad Zwischenahn. The fighter took off on a jettisonable trolley and landed on a retractable skid. The Komet, which possessed a fantastic rate of climb and a top speed of around 600mph, went into service as a target-defence interceptor, but remained extremely dangerous to its pilots. A Me 163B is here shown starting up and taking off.

Above left: Oberstleutnant Graf, Geschwaderkommodore of JG 11, with Hauptmann Hermichen, Kommandeur of I./JG 11, spring 1944.
Above right: Major Günther Specht, Kommandeur of II./JG 11, with Staffelkapitän Oberleutnant Sommer and Professor Kurt Tank, designer of the Fw 190.
Below: Here they come! Swarms of U.S. bombers leave a trail of devastation and sorrow in their wake.

Above left: Oberfeldwebel Adolf Glunz has just brought down another heavy bomber. These were to account for twenty of his seventy-one victories.
Above right: Rocket-armed Bf 110G–2s of 6./ZG 76 form up to attack the bombers, early 1944.
Left: Two aces of JG 26: Oberleutnant Alfred Heckmann, Kapitän of 3. Staffel, and Oberfeldwebel Adolf Glunz, Kapitan of 5. Staffel.

Above left: Hauptmann Kiel, Staffelkapitän of 7./ZG 26, supervises the loading of the rocket launchers on his Bf 110G–2.
Above right: The firing of a Werfer-Granate 21 (air-to-air rocket).
Bottom: A detailed shot of a Bf 110G–2/R3/U9 carrying four Werfer-Granate 21s, a twin-gun Rüstsatz (armament pod) and two 300-litre drop tanks.

Above: The Kommodore of JG 2, Oberstleutnant Egon Mayer, examines a B-17 which he has brought down. At the beginning of 1944, he was the most successful heavy bomber specialist. He was killed in combat with Thunderbolts near Montmedy on 2 March 1944, with a tally of 102 enemy aircraft, of which twenty-five were four-engined bombers.
Below left: Oberleutnant Herbert Huppertz of II./JG 2, May 1944. Huppertz was another Thunderbolt victim, on 8 June 1944. His victories totalled sixty-eight.
Below right: Generalfeldmarschall Erwin Rommel visits JG 26 in May 1944, just before the invasion.

Top: Young pilots of JG 104 with their Bf 109G–6s. The training given at the fighter-conversion schools was thorough, but the shortage of fuel and the high attrition rate in the fighter units led to ever fewer flying hours per student. Many a new pilot did not survive his first operational sortie.

Middle and bottom: Bf 109G–6s and G–14s of JG 104 on a training flight. This was still possible in April 1944, before the Allies' air superiority became too great.

Above left: Major Walter Dahl, seen here as Kommandeur of III./JG 3 in early 1944, was given the task in May 1944 of forming a special-purpose Jagdgeschwader. The IVth Gruppe, known as the Sturmgruppe, was best employed against the bomber streams. In the battle over Oschersleben on 7 July 1944, the Sturmjäger, in a wedge formation, scattered the American bombers, and the IVth Gruppe, led by Hauptmann Moritz, claimed thirty bombers shot down.

In January 1945, Dahl was appointed Inspekteur der Tagjäger (Inspector of Day Fighters). He obtained a total of 128 victories, of which thirty-six were heavy bombers.

Above right: An artist's impression of a 'Rammjäger' attack.

Below: An Fw 190A–8/R2 of a Sturmgruppe (ground attack group).

III./JG 3 and their leader, Hauptmann Karl-Heinz Langer (below, right). This unit was assigned to the z.b.V. (Special Purpose Jagdgeschwader) in May 1944, and subsequently to JG 300.

Above and below: Fw 190A–8/R2s of Sturmgruppe IV./JG 3 at Schongau, August 1944.

Above: Hauptmann Moritz, Kommandeur of IV./Sturm/JG 3, and his Fw 190A–8/R2.
Below: A Schwarm of Bf 109G–6/R2s of I./JG 5 under Hauptmann Theo Weissenberger is scrambled, invasion front 1944.

Above left: A Bf 109G–10/R3 makes its final approach before landing.
Above right: Hauptmann Weissenberger after a hard sortie.
Below: American escort fighters lie in wait for rash German attackers.

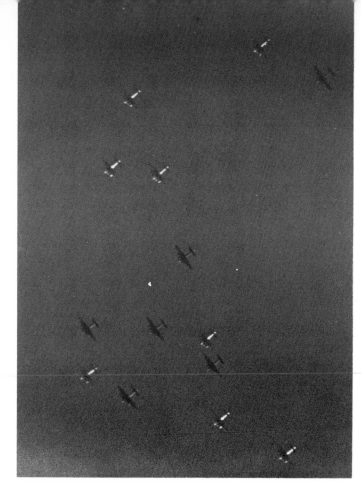

Above left: A formation of Flying Fortresses on their way to attack a German city; an almost daily sight in 1944.

Above right: Leutnant Oskar Romm on leave after receiving his Ritterkreuz for seventy-six victories, 29 February 1944. From early 1944, Romm flew with IV./Sturm/JG 3, and on 27 September 1944 he shot down three Liberators in one sortie. On 18 February 1945, he was appointed leader of his Gruppe.

Below: In November 1944, Leutnant 'Ossi' Romm as Kapitän of 4./JG 3 was flying this Bf 109G–10/U2, a high-altitude version.

Above: Generalfeldmarschall Sperrle chose to visit Major Heinz Bär's II./JG 1 in the summer of 1944. What he found does not appear to have been to his liking.
Below: I./JG 27 scramble in Austria, autumn 1944.

Right: This wedge was used for breaking into a bomber formation and dispersing it.
Below: Berlin in flames after a heavy bombing raid in the winter of 1944–45.

Right: Bf 109Gs of I./JG 27 on an airfield in Germany.
Below: Immeasurable grief and sorrow for the people in the cities.

Above left: Both the size and the armament of the B-17G were impressive.
Above right: 'Deadeye' 750 shot down after twenty-five missions.
Below: A conference of Kommodoren: G. Rödel (JG 27), H. Bär (JG 1) and K. Bühligen (JG 2).

Above left: Major Toni Hackl, Kommandeur of III./JG 11, after achieving about 150 victories in July 1944. By the war's end, Hackl had amassed 192 victories, including thirty-two heavy bombers, in over 1,000 sorties.
Above right: A Boeing B-17G on fire.
Below: Major Kurt Bühligen, last Kommodore of JG 2 'Richthofen,' on the occasion of his 100th victory, 9 June 1944.

Major Schöpfel, Kommodore of JG 4, in his Fw 190A–4, summer 1944.

Hauptmann Rolf Hermichen, Kommandeur of I./JG 11, was one of the Luftwaffe's most successful pilots for shooting down bombers; his sixty-four victories included twenty-six bombers.

Left: Oberstleutnant Priller's 100th victory, on 2 July 1944, was a Liberator. At left is Hauptmann Matoni.
Bottom: Priller and other fighter pilots of I./JG 2 before a sortie.

Opposite page: An artist's impression of a Flying Fortress succumbing to attacking Fw 190s, 1944.
This page: A Typhoon 1B of 44 (Canadian) Squadron attacks a convoy.

Right: Oberstleutnant Josef Priller explains the head-on attack to new pilots.

Below: III./JG 54 converted to Fw 190A–7s in the summer of 1944. This picture shows them at Oldenburg in September of that year.

Left: Major Toni Hackl, Kommandeur of II./JG 26 from October 1944.
Below: A Bf 109G–6/R3 on duty in defence of the Reich.

Right: Major Klaus Mietusch, Kommandeur of III./JG 26, was fatally wounded by Mustangs while landing at Aldekerk on 17 September 1944. He was awarded a posthumous Eichenlaub for his seventy-two victories.

Below: A Spitfire IX sweeps in to the attack.

Above left: Trucks burn after a British fighter-bomber attack.
Above right: The scattered wreckage of an Fw 190.
Below: Victims of an air raid laid out for identification in the exhibition hall at the Funkturm (Radio Tower), Berlin 1944–45.

The end of an American bomber crew after fifty-four missions.

Top: A Bf 109G–10 Staffel is scrambled ... *Middle:* ... and hurls itself at the enemy.
Bottom: Whether in piston or jet aircraft, the German pilots fought against overwhelming superiority of numbers, and succeeded or died.

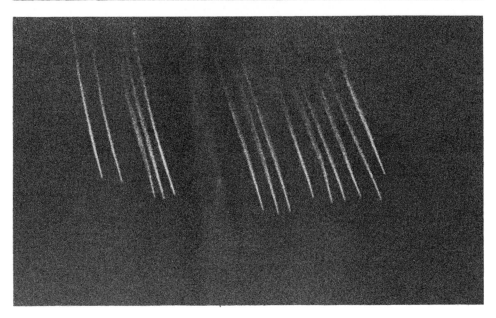

Above: Bf 109G–6s of JG 53.
Below: An Fw 190A–7/R6 is loaded with 21cm. rockets.

Top: Oberfeldwebel Hermann Buchner, a former ground-attack pilot, with forty-six victories, went on to shoot down twelve heavy bombers with the Me 262A–1.
Middle: An Me 262 unit at Lechfeld.
Bottom: The last photograph of Hauptmann Robert Weiss, Kommandeur of III./JG 54, who was killed fighting against overwhelming odds on 29 December 1944.

Right: A Kette (formation of three) of Fw 190Gs. German fighters, often operating in small groups, frequently succeeded in penetrating the screen of hundreds of fighters surrounding the bombers.
Below: Separated bombers especially fell prey to German fighters. This B-17 is about to go down.

Above: American and British fighter-bombers forced the German fighters into hiding.
Below: The end of the road for a Spitfire XIX of 350 (Belgian) Squadron.

Right: General 'Beppo' Schmid, commander of the 1st Jagdkorps, has called his Geschwader leaders together. At his side is General Galland, without his medals, which he has removed in protest at Göring's incompetence.

Below: Front row: Falck, Huth, Trautloft, Hajo Herrmann. Behind Falck is Hauptmann Albrecht, and beyond him is Hauptmann Eder.

In the last weeks of the war Fw 190s operated mainly as fighter-bombers. These Fw 190F–8/R13s are loaded with SC bombs (Spreng Cylindrisch or General Purpose) and double drop tanks in preparation for an attack on Allied armour.

Above: Fw 190F–8/R 13s warming up their engines, under the cover of trees.

Above: Fw 190D–9s of the Stabsschwarm (Staff Flight) of IV./JG 3 under Oberleutnant 'Ossi' Romm at Prenzlau, near Berlin, March 1945.

Above: P–38 Lightnings attacking ground targets, 1945.

Above: A P-47D Thunderbolt shoots-up a German airfield.

The end of the once-strong Luftwaffe . . . A treasure-trove for souvenir-hunters.